Please Enjoy!

THE FOUR SISTERS

Norma Naranjo

The Feasting Place

Ohkay Owingeh Pueblo

Table Of Contents

Acknowledgments

This book would not be possible without the help of our ancestors, who have passed down the knowledge, wisdom, and most importantly, our culture and traditions. We have been blessed with the support of our families and friends. We wish to thank all the people who have tasted and tested our recipes.

We would like to give a special thank you to Alice Loy for encouraging us to do this cookbook. We would also like to thank her daughter, Macy Loy, for taking on the challenging task of designing this book, and Liz Brindley for illustrating this book. Additionally, thank you to my daughter, Nina Valdez, and her friend Brittany, for contributing the photos.

This book is also in memory of my grandmother, Rosalia, my mother Margaret, and my mothers-in-law, Candy Naranjo and Grace Valdez, for contributing their recipes.

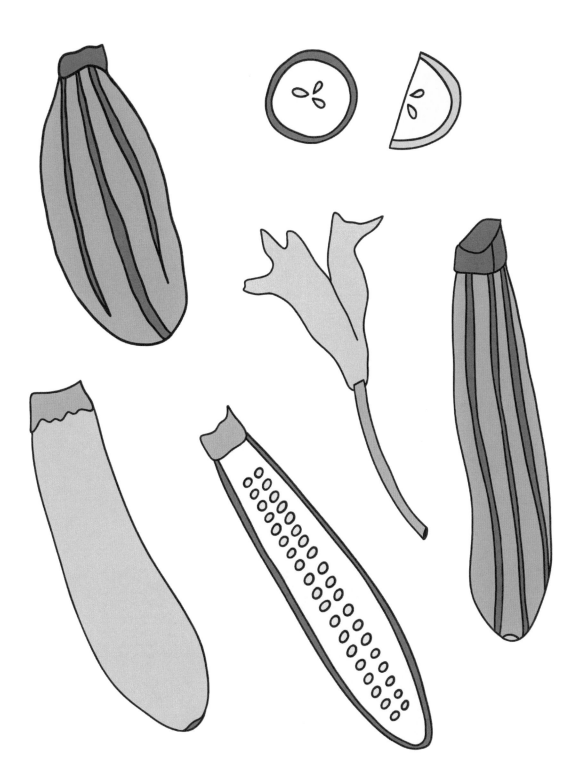

THE FOUR SISTERS

Norma Naranjo
Ohkay Owingeh Pueblo

Preface

The Four Sisters is a collection of recipes and their stories from my life in Ohkay Owingeh, one of the Eight Tewa Pueblos in Northern New Mexico. I started The Feasting Place in 2000 to share traditional cooking with friends and loved ones. Now that group of friends and loved ones has expanded and includes people from all over the world!

The Feasting Place is located in our cozy, vibrant pueblo home on The Pueblo's tribal lands and offers a view of the beautiful Sangre de Cristo Mountains rising above the cooking ovens, or *hornos*, in our backyard. Hornos are traditional adobe ovens where Pueblo people do our baking, especially for feast days and other traditional holidays. The baking and cooking done in the outside hornos is a place to share old family recipes and bring family and friends together for memorable times. As I write this, the fire is in the horno, and the bread is almost ready to bake!

The Feasting Place brings hopes of sharing culture and tradition, creating a lasting connection of earth and spirit. The Four Sisters is really what food is all about: not only does food nourish the body, but it feeds our spirit, especially in the company of loved ones. Please enjoy this book of recipes and their stories as much as I have loved putting them together for you.

And, if you are ever in Northern New Mexico, please come by The Feasting Place and share some food and wonderful times with my family and me!

Introduction

I am from Ohkay Owingeh, formerly known as San Juan Pueblo, nestled in the foothills of the mountains north of Santa Fe, New Mexico. I am the second to the oldest of six children; one of my brothers died in 2015. I am the oldest of four sisters and, now one brother. My father was an enrolled tribal member of Ohkay Owingeh and my mother was Hispanic; she grew up in Ohkay Owingeh.

I graduated in 1969 from Española High in Española, New Mexico. After graduation, I joined the Navy during the Vietnam War. After serving three years in the Navy, I started my higher education on the GI Bill, at the College of Santa Fe, graduating in 1976 with a Bachelor's Degree in Social Work. I continued my education on the GI Bill, earning a Master's in Social Work from Highlands University in Las Vegas, New Mexico in 1981.

I married and had two children, Nina and Pedro, who are the joy of my life. I also have three wonderful grandchildren: Eliseo, DJ, and Amalia, whom I adore. I remarried in 1988 to Eugene "Hutch" Naranjo who has been an integral part of our lives. During the course of my career, I worked for the US Public Health Corps, working for Indian Health Service and Rural Health. I retired in 1999 from the U.S. Public Health Corps and that is when my second career started.

I started my small business in the year 2000 out of our home in Ohkay Owingeh. The name of my business is The Feasting Place. I learned to cook from my mother and grandmother who helped me master the art of baking in the horno.

We are four sisters in our family which I relate to the three sisters, beans, squash, corn and lastly the fourth sister which is the chile that is a staple in every Pueblo home during feast days. Also, there are four seasons. As the four seasons of our lives change, so does our response to the spirits' greatness of newness, beauty, and hope for ourselves, our families, and communities. The four directions also symbolize how our creator takes care of all his people through the North, West, South, and East which typically represent the colors of corn: red, blue, yellow, and white. That is how I came up with the title of this cookbook, "The Four Sisters".

My legacy lies on the strength of my ancestors through traditional values and foods, and a woven blend of my Native and Hispanic cultures. Growing up in the Pueblo, participating in our traditional songs, dances and feasts, I was able to absorb the wisdom of my elders. Today, I share this wisdom and our traditions, and the legacy of my grandmother and mother with my guests through my cooking and these recipes.

Memories of Our Horno

The horno is an outdoor oven that Pueblo people have used to bake our bread for centuries. It's made out of adobe mud and has a beehive shape. The horno is used throughout the Pueblos of New Mexico. My first memories of using the horno are when I was about eight years old. My mom started teaching me how to make the dough in the evening and we would get up early to start the fire after chopping the wood. I remember the crackling sound of the cedar wood as the horno was heating. It smelled good, too.

My mother taught me how to roll out the dough and make beautiful shapes for the bread. It was laid out on the tables to rise. Then, I observed how to make pies and cookies. As children, with my brothers and sisters, we helped in the kitchen, took out the bread and the pies and cookies to bake, and helped clean up. Those were our chores. That was the hard part-when we had to help before we could eat! We always knew when we smelled the bread nearly ready to come out that our reward was coming for all our hard work!

My three sisters and I still carry on the tradition of baking bread, pies and cookies. Our children and grandchildren come to help as we did as children. My husband, Hutch, and my grandson, chop the wood and have it ready to start the fire. It is experiencing déjà vu all over again by carrying on the tradition with our children and grandchildren.

Hutch learned how to build hornos from my stepfather, Tomas. Now we have two hornos in our backyard we use to bake and cook. Hutch has built several hornos throughout Northern New Mexico. Together, we hold classes throughout the year and we teach people from all over the world how to cook and bake in the horno.

Norma's Horno Bread

5 pounds all-purpose flour
½ cup shortening
1 package yeast - approximately 1 tablespoon
4 cups warm water
2 tablespoons salt
1 tablespoon sugar

I recommend using aluminum baking pans.

Preheat oven to 400 degrees. Mix flour, shortening, and salt together in a large bowl. In a separate bowl mix approximately 4 warm cups of water, yeast and sugar. Let stand for 10 minutes.

Slowly add the 4 cups of water mixture to the flour mixture and mix using your hands until the mix forms a ball. Start kneading the dough until the dough starts springing back. Then coat the dough with shortening, cover with dish towel, set on the counter, and let the dough rise for 2 hours in a warm place.

Once the dough has risen, knead the dough for two minutes. Do not over knead the dough. Divide up the dough into five equal amounts and form into individual loaves. Put the loaves into aluminum pans and let rise for 1 hour, or until the loaves double in size.

Bake for 40 minutes in an horno or a conventional oven at 400 degrees for 55 minutes. Depending on your oven, you can lower the temperature to 350 degrees.

Makes approximately 5 loaves.

Winter

This is my favorite time of the year. It's a time to be thankful for the abundance of a wonderful harvest. The Sangre de Cristo Mountains I can see from my kitchen window are snowcapped in the distance. It's a time to slow down and sit by the crackling fire after preserving our native crops and all the intense labor.

As a child, growing up in Ohkay Owingeh, I remember the first snowfalls of the winter. I knew Christmas was coming and the family would soon be gathering to celebrate the holidays. My mother and my aunts would come together to bake bread, pies, cookies, and make tamales. There would be laughter and catching up with our cousins. My siblings and I would go to the Pueblo's main Plaza to see the Matachine dancers and stay for Vespers in the evening. We would return to help my mother cook for our Christmas Day on December 26th, the day we celebrate the Turtle Dance. The Turtle Dance is a beautiful dance with the rhythm of only the sound of deer hooves on the turtle shell and the men singing to the spirits, thanking them for a wonderful year.

People would come to our home and feast with all the wonderful dishes my mother had prepared on December 26th. I remember entering our home or walking around the Pueblo Plaza to be greeted with an aroma of stews simmering. I would be ready to sit down to enjoy a steaming bowl of stew with Pueblo bread. I also remember the smell of piñon. Piñon brings home the holiday spirit as our family gathers for the holidays. The smell of piñon wood burning in the fireplaces, with the aroma of piñon nuts roasting in the oven, brings such unforgetable memories.

I remember during my childhood going on long expedition rides to the mountains to pick piñon nuts. It was a family affair. My siblings and I would race to see who would pick the most nuts by the time lunch came around. My brother would climb a tree and shake it fiercely. The nuts would fall and we would rush to pick them. We would have to give him some of our piñon nuts for his labor. That is how he would be the winner, with the most piñon nuts in his bag!

My mom would store the piñon nuts in a flour sack and later would roast them for different recipes. I have continued the traditions of baking and cooking which I credit my mother and grandmother for teaching me.

Photo credit: Alfredo Montoya

Pork Tamales

Red Chile Sauce:
4 ounces Chile Caribe, available online
4 cups warm water
3 cloves garlic or 1 teaspoon garlic powder
1 to 2 teaspoons salt

Place chile into a pot and boil. After the chile is soft, put in a blender along with garlic, salt, and water. Blend until liquefied and then cook for 15 more minutes.

Tamale Dough:
2 cups tamale cornmeal flour, also known as "masa"
1 teaspoon salt
¾ cup lard or vegetable shortening
2 cups broth from meat (hot)
You may add more water if the dough gets too dry.

Tamale Filling:
1½ pounds pork shoulder
6 to 8 cups water
2 teaspoons salt

Place pork in a pot, add water and salt, and cover. Bring to a boil. Reduce heat to medium and continue to cook until fork tender. 2-3hours. Set broth aside for tamale dough. Shred meat and place in a bowl. Add chile sauce to pork, soak dried corn husk in a pan with hot water for 15 minutes.

With a spoon, spread tamale dough evenly over the husk. Place 2 tbs of meat filling. Wrap the husk around the tamale and tie end with string of corn husk. Place tamales in a steamer pot with hot water, cover, and steam for 45 to 50 minutes.

Makes approximately 2 to 3 dozen tamales.

Norma's Blue Corn Muffins

1 cup blue corn meal
1 cup all-purpose flour
1 teaspoon baking soda
1 teaspoon salt
¼ cup sugar
1 cup buttermilk
4 tablespoons vegetable oil
1 egg
¼ to ½ cup pine nuts (optional)

Mix blue corn meal, all purpose flour, baking soda, salt. In a separate mixing bowl, mix egg, add sugar, buttermilk, and vegetable oil. Add into dry ingredients and mix well. Add pine nuts and mix. Spray muffin pan and pour the batter in each pan cup ¾ full. Bake at 400 degrees for 18 to 20 minutes. Enjoy with home made preserves, honey or butter.

Makes approximately 12 muffins.

Bread Pudding

1 loaf white bread (toasted)
2 cups Longhorn Cheese, shredded
1½ teaspoons cinnamon
2½ cups sugar (add sprinkling of water as needed)
2 tablespoons vanilla
Raisins and pine nuts are optional

Preheat over to 325 degrees.

In a deep pan, layer bread, cheese, raisins, and piñon nuts. Sprinkle cinnamon on toasted bread. Brown 2½ cups of sugar slowly until caramelized. Sprinkle in water slowly to make a thin syrup.

Add vanilla. Pour boiling syrup all over until all the bread is absorbed. Place in oven at 325 degrees until cheese has melted.

Serves approximately 8 to 10.

Atole

4 cups water
1 cup blue corn meal

Boil 3 cups water of water. Bring to a rapid boil. Dissolve blue corn meal in 1 cup cold water.

Slowly add blue cornmeal (in water) to boiling water and whisk rapidly until it comes to a semi thick consistency.

Note: This drink can be flavored with milk, sugar, salt, or honey.

Serves approximately 6.

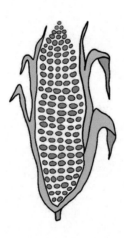

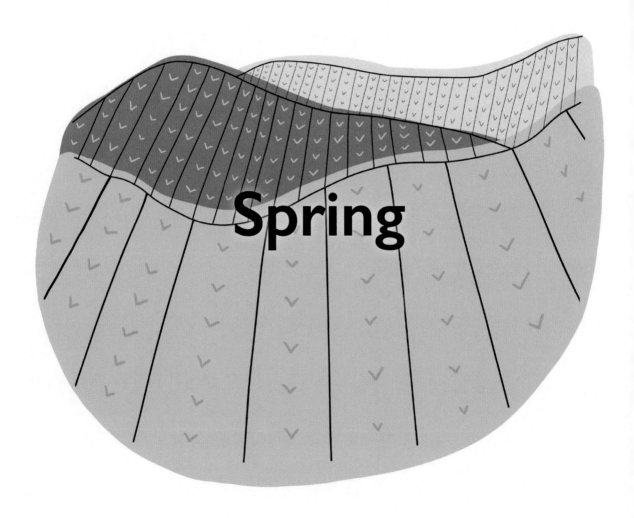

Spring

Spring is the time when Mother Earth is preparing herself for a cleansing and getting ready for a new growing season. It's a celebration of all the different herbs (chimaha, wild asparagus, wild onions) cultivating themselves to be picked later in the spring.

During my growing up in Ohkay Owingeh, I remember the days when the men from the Pueblo would gather behind our home to clean the ditch, or *acequia*, which would supply the irrigation water for our gardens and corn fields. The men in our family would begin to plow and cultivate the fields and get them ready for planting.

The women from Ohkay Owingeh would prepare food for the men who would break for lunch. Some of the dishes my mother would prepare included a big pot of pinto beans that had been boiling since early morning to be ready for lunch. My mother would also prepare a pot of green chile stew. I remember helping my mother make a big batch of fry bread (kap owanu). She would roll the dough and I would turn the bread frying in the oil. I still remember the smell in the kitchen. This tradition is still carried on today.

During springtime we would also get ready for Lent. Here are some Lenten foods prepared during Lent.

Yellow Split Pea Soup

2½ cups dried yellow split peas
8 cups water
1 medium onion, diced
1 teaspoon garlic powder
Salt to taste

Place dried peas along with water in a crock pot and place on high for 5 hours. You can add more water as needed. Once pea soup is done, saute onion, add garlic powder and salt. Mix together. We usually put vegetarian red chile in the soup and the herb chimaha.

Chimaha is an herb that grows wild in the sandy foothills in northern New Mexico during early spring. It resembles parsley and oregano. When picked you wash and put it out to dry. It is used in scrambled eggs, beans, or soups.

This is a soup my grandmother would always cook during Lent season.

Serves approximately 6 to 8.

Pinto Beans

3 cups pinto beans
7 cups water
Salt to taste

Clean and wash the pinto beans and soak overnight. Place the beans in a slow cooker with 7 cups of water. Cook for 4 to 5 hours.

Optional: You may add ham hocks, diced ham, bacon, or *chicos* for flavor and texture. Add salt to taste.

Serves approximately 8 to 10.

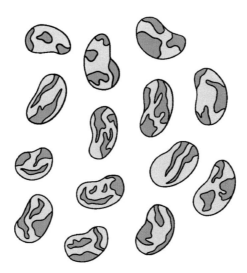

Torta de Huevo

20 red chile pods, dried
4 cups water
3 tablespoons flour
3 tablespoons cooking oil
3 cloves garlic, minced
4 eggs
Salt to taste

Remove seeds and stems from chile pods, wash and pat dry. Place chiles on a sheet pan and bake at 400 degrees until the pods are soft. Place chiles in a blender with water until they become pureed. Mix flour, oil and brown. Add chile puree, bring to a boil until it is the consistency of gravy. Add garlic and salt to taste and simmer for 30 minutes.

Separate eggs, beat egg yolks, beat egg whites until stiff, fold in egg yolks. Drop mixture by tablespoons into hot oil and brown on both sides. Drain on paper towels, add to red chile.

This dish is usually made during Lent season and is usually served with pinto beans or salmon patties.

Serves approximately 8.

21

Panocha

5 cups panocha flour, also known as sprouted wheat flour
2½ cups whole wheat flour
2 cups sugar
9 cups boiling water
4 tablespoons butter (optional)

Preheat oven to 250 degrees.

Add half of boiling water to flour in a pan and let rest for 15 minutes. Caramelize the sugar on medium heat, and stir until the sugar has completely melted and come to a brown color. Add the other half of boiling water to sugar and mix. Add sugar mixture to the mixed flour and mix. Put in the oven for 2 hours at 250 degrees and stir occasionally. It will become thick at the end. Lastly, you may add butter and vanilla to your taste. Can be served alone or with whip cream.

This recipe is my children's grandmother, Grace Valdez. She always made this recipe during Lent season. I use this recipe with some adjustment for traditional ceremonies and bake it in the horno.

Serves approximately 24.

Indian Fry Bread

2½ pounds shortening or coconut oil
4 cups sifted flour
3 tablespoons baking powder
1 tablespoons salt
5 tablespoons shortening
2 cups warm water

Melt shortening or coconut oil in a deep pot. Combine flour, baking powder, shortening and salt in a large mixing bowl. Add warm water in small amounts until it comes together. Dough should be soft and manageable but not sticky.

Make egg-sized balls of dough and let stand for about 5 minutes. Roll out into rounds about half an inch thick with a rolling pin. Pierce hole in the center of each round and place into hot grease until it puffs fry quickly and turn over and fry on the other side until golden brown.

Serves approximately 8 to 10.

Summer

Summer is when you began to see the fresh greens for salads and the pleasure of seeing results of all the seeds you planted in the spring.

Summer was a season that had mixed emotions for me. I was happy that school was over for the year, but knew that there was hard work ahead. Growing up in Ohkay Owingeh, we always had a big garden and big corn fields. That meant all my siblings and I would need to get up early to hoe the garden or irrigate the long rows of corn.

It was always exciting in June to look forward to our Feast Day on June 24th. Once again, my family would come together to bake and cook. We would look forward to going to the carnival and eating burgers from Rosie's Burger Stand. My siblings and I would hang out to see the dances and mingle with the crowd at the arts and crafts stands. Later, we would return home to help our mom serve our guests with fresh Indian mint tea and all the Feast food.

As I became older, I wanted to experience baking bread in the horno on my own. As I've described, I mastered the art of baking in the horno from my grandma and mom. I learned that mastering the art of horno baking requires trial and error. My first batch of bread was a disaster! It came out hard and flat. My family refused to eat the bread so I had to throw it away. My grandmother came to the rescue and helped me bake another batch of bread and that is when I understood the art of mixing the dough and firing the horno. The rest is history.

My three sisters and I still come together to carry on the legacy of our grandmother and mother by cooking and baking for Feast Day on June 24th. Each of my sisters brings her favorite dish and helps throughout the day.

Raisin Drop Cookies

1 cup raisins
½ cup water
1 cup white sugar
½ cup shortening
3 eggs
1 teaspoon vanilla
2 cups flour
½ teaspoon baking soda
½ teaspoon salt
½ teaspoon cinnamon
½ teaspoon baking powder
1 cup nuts (any type) or coconut

Boil raisins in water for 5 minutes until the water has evaporated. Set aside.

Using an electric mixer, cream together the white sugar and shortening. Then, while mixing on low, add 3 eggs, one at a time. Add vanilla and raisins.

Add dry ingredients to the wet mixture and mix together on low. Fold in 1 cup chopped nuts or coconut. Place parchment paper on a cookie sheet. With a small melon scooper, drop cookie dough on the cookie sheet and place 2 inches apart. Cookie dough will spread a little.

Bake at 425 degrees for 12 to 15 minutes. Let cool.

Makes approximately 6 dozen.

Mae's Potato Salad

5 pounds bag red potatoes
6 hard boiled eggs
1 cup chopped celery
2 tablespoons dill pickle relish
1 tablespoon chopped green onions
1 4 ounce jar of diced pimientos
1 tablespoon yellow mustard
1½ cup mayonnaise (add more if needed)
Salt and pepper to taste

Wash and peel potatoes. Cut potatoes into ¼ inch cubes. Boil potatoes until tender. Boil eggs for 9 to 12 minutes. While potatoes are cooking, chop celery and green onion. Peel eggs, place egg yolk in a small bowl and chop the egg whites. Combine cooked potatoes, eggs, celery, pimientos, green onion, olives, and dill relish. Mix all together. In a small bowl, mash cooked egg yolk and add a small squirt of mustard. Mix well with mayonnaise. Add mayonnaise mixture to potato mixture and mix well. Add salt and pepper to taste. Refrigerate.

Serves approximately 10.

In the past recent years, potato salad has become a staple on Feast Days.

This is my second oldest sister, Mae's recipe.

Cookie's Jello Mold

2 cups water
One 6 ounce box orange jello
One 15 ounce can mandarin oranges
One 8 ounce tub Cool Whip

Bring water to a boil. In a large bowl, mix jello powder and boiling water until well dissolved. Add thawed (room temperature) Cool Whip and stir into hot jello mixture until it is all dissolved.

Drain the juice from the mandarin oranges and stir in mandarin oranges to jello mixture and mix all together. Pour into a jello mold. Chill overnight.

To loosen jello from the mold, soak mold in hot water for one minute. Place a large serving platter or plate over the mold and quickly flip both to pull jello out of mold.

Serves approximately 8 to 10.

This recipe is always served on Feast Days or other traditional holidays!

This is my youngest sister, Cookie's, recipe.

Norma's Red Chile

2 pounds boneless pork stew meat
3 to 4 cups cold water
½ cup red powered chile
5 medium potatoes, peeled and cubed
Salt to taste

In a saucepan, put stew meat and cold water. Bring to a boil and simmer for about one hour or until tender. Boil potatoes in another pot until potatoes are cooked. Place potatoes into cooked meat. Add chile and bring to a boil for approximately 30 minutes. Add salt to taste.

Serves approximately 4 to 6.

Norma's Pie Dough

1 pound Crisco shortening or lard
5 cups all purpose flour
1 cup ice cold water
1 teaspoon vinegar

Cut/mix Crisco into flour. Combine water and vinegar and add to the flour shortening mix. Knead very gently until mixture comes together. Can be put into the refrigerator for 15 to 30 minutes. Roll out into a pie pan.

Indian Taco

10 to 12 pieces of Fry bread (see fry bread recipe on page 36)
1 pound ground beef
¼ cup ground red chile
4 cups cooked pinto beans (cooked or canned)
2 cups shredded lettuce
2 cups shredded cheddar cheese
1 cup chopped onions
1 cup diced tomatoes
2 cups water
1 teaspoon garlic salt
1 teaspoon onion powder
1 teaspoon salt

In a frying pan, add ground meat, cook until completely browned. Use a slotted spoon to take out any grease. Add red chile to ground cooked meat and water and simmer for 30 minutes. Add garlic salt, onion powder and salt. You may add to pinto beans or serve the beans and the meat separately.

Spoon the beans and red ground beef chile on top of a freshly made fry bread. Top with cheese, lettuce, tomatoes, and onions.

Serves approximately 10 to 12.

Norma's Indian Pueblo Cookies (Bûuʔtsí)

6 eggs
2 cups sugar
1 pound lard
¼ cup vanilla extract
3½ tablespoons baking powder
8 cups flour

Sugar Mixture:
1 cup sugar
1 tablespoon cinnamon

Preheat oven to 350 degrees.

Mix lard and sugar until well mixed. I mix by hand. Add eggs and mix thoroughly, add vanilla, flour, and baking powder to the mixture a little at a time until dough comes together. You may add more flour if still sticky. Add flour to the surface and roll out with a rolling pin until dough is about ¼ inch thick. Cut into shapes with a cookie cutter and dip into cinnamon sugar mixture. Bake in the horno for 5 minutes or conventional oven for 10 minutes at 350 degrees.

Makes approximately 8 dozen.

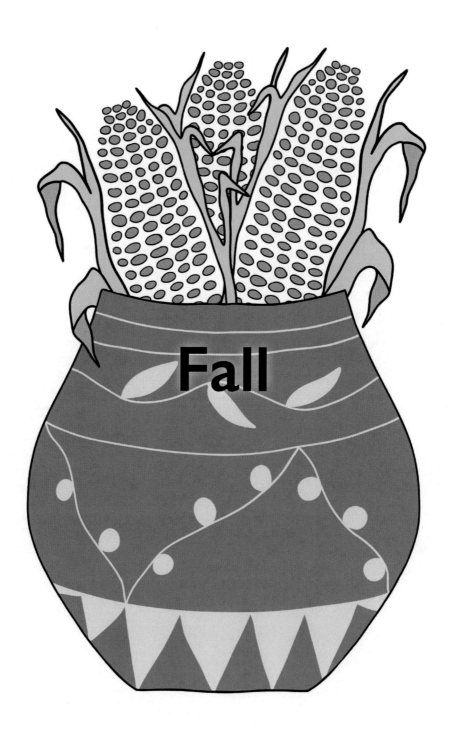

Fall

Fall is a season that lets you know you have mastered the art of producing the beautiful four sisters: corn, chile, squash, beans and all the other vegetables you may have planted in the spring. Fall is a season that you celebrate with songs, dance and prayers. It reminds us of a time to understand that we have had an intimate relationship with Mother Earth and water.

As a child growing up in Ohkay Owingeh, I remember the aroma of Mother Earth during the monsoon season, the green chile and corn roasting in the horno. People from the village would come together to harvest the bountiful crops of corn to husk and make "chicos".

Chicos have become a delicacy because of the intense labor it requires to harvest and husk. Also, the chico corn is hard to find. Some people make their chicos with sweet corn. Chico is a small white corn that is grown in Northern New Mexico. It is a corn that must be picked at a time when the kernels still have milk. If the kernel becomes hard it is not good for chicos. You can roast the corn in the horno by leaving it overnight to roast. In the morning you take it out of the horno and hang the corn with the husk to dry. Or, you can husk the corn and boil it in a big aluminum tub over a fire, removing the kernels once they are soft and then putting them on a wire rack to dry.

Once the kernels are dried, you remove them from the cob and clean them with a screen. Many Pueblo people cook chicos with various types of meat: pork, beef, or game. We also add them to pinto beans and serve during feast days and traditional holidays.

I also remember the fall season when the men from the village would go hunting for turkey, deer, and elk. The women would stay home to preserve the bountiful foods from the garden by drying, canning, and freezing to sustain the family and community for another cycle of life.

Chico Stew

1 pound dry chicos
2 to 2 1/2 pounds stew meat (beef, pork, or short ribs)
8 to 10 cups water
1 medium yellow onion
1 tablespoon garlic salt
Salt to taste

Dice onion. Then, put dry chicos, stew meat, diced onion, and water in a crock pot. Cook for 6 hours. (Note: You may need to add more water throughout the cooking process.) When cooked, add garlic and salt to taste.

Makes approximately 6 servings.

Norma's Green Chile Stew

1 pound ground beef
5 potatoes (medium to large)
15 medium green chilies roasted, peeled, seeded and chopped
2 cloves garlic, diced
1 medium onion, diced
Salt to taste
6 cups water

Brown the ground beef thoroughly and then drain off the grease. Add diced onion and garlic to ground beef and saute for 5 minutes. Add water and potatoes to meat. Add chopped green chile to potatoes and meat. Boil for 15 minutes or until soft. Add salt to taste.

Serves approximately 6 to 8.

Picadillo

4 large apples, any kind of apples that are in season
4 fresh green chiles, not roasted
1 onion
1 cucumber
½ cup apple cider vinegar
¼ cup water
2 tablespoons sugar
1 jalapeño chile (optional)
6 radishes

Cut apples, fresh green chiles, cucumbers, and onions into small diced size. Slice radishes thinly and put all vegetables in a bowl and serve with dressing.

Dressing:
In a small bowl add apple cider vinegar, water and sugar. Mix thoroughly and put on vegetables and refrigerate for approximately 1 hour before serving.

This recipe is over a hundred years old. It came from my children's great-great grandfather who was a farmer in Velarde, New Mexico. He would make this recipe when the apples, cucumber, and chile were in season. He would pick everything fresh from the garden. This recipe is usually eaten with pinto beans and fresh tortillas.

Serves approximately 6 to 8.

Watermelon Salad

4 cups fresh cut watermelon
1 smal package spinach
1 small package arugula
1 small container feta cheese
½ cup roasted pine nuts
¼ cup torn mint

Dressing:
3 tablespoons extra virgin olive oil
2 tablespoons lime juice
1 garlic, minced
¼ teaspoon salt

Make dressing: In a small mason jar, put olive oil, lime juice, garlic and salt. Shake the jar until everything is mixed.

Mix Spinach, arugula, and watermelon in a bowl or platter and drizzle half of the dressing. Top with feta cheese, mint, and pine nuts. Drizzle the remaining dressing. Season with salt to taste and serve.

Serves approximately 4 to 6.

Poor Man Tacos

1 pound ground beef
1 teaspoon salt
2 cloves garlic, minced
1 small onion, diced
3 tablespoons fresh cilantro, chopped
1 small package frozen peas
8 corn tortillas
¼ cup cooking oil
¼ head lettuce, chopped
2 medium tomatoes diced
1½ cups cheddar or jack cheese
1 small onion, chopped (optional)

Brown the ground beef, add diced onion and garlic saute for 4 minutes, add peas to ground beef and stir for 2 minutes. Remove pan from heat and add cilantro.

Fry your corn tortillas and make your tacos adding ground beef, along with lettuce, tomatoes, cheese, and onions if you want more. You can add salsa from the store or make your own (see Salsa recipe below on page 67).

This recipe is my children's grandmother's, Grace Valdez. She would make these tacos for the family and the story she would tell was that they were called "poor man tacos" because "back in the day," people had big families so in order to make a meal with the tacos she would add more ingredients like peas to make them go a long way. However true her story may be, the family still enjoys these delicious tacos!

Serves approximately 8.

Toma's Salsa Recipe

One 14 ounce can of whole tomatoes
3 stems of green onions
1 to 2 jalapenos
1 cup cilantro
1 teaspoon salt
1 teaspoon garlic salt

Put all the ingredients in a food processor and mix until everything has purified and come together. It is wonderful with chips or on tacos.

Makes approximately 16 servings.

This is my second youngest sister, Toma's, recipe.

Zucchini Bread

Wet Ingredients:
1½ cup grated zucchini
1 cup sugar
¼ cup brown sugar
½ cup unsweetened apple sauce
⅓ cup vegetable oil
2 large eggs
1 teaspoon vanilla

Dry Ingredients:
1½ cup flour
½ teaspoon baking powder
½ teaspoon baking soda
½ teaspoon salt
½ teaspoon cinnamon
1 cup nuts

Preheat oven to 350 degrees. Grease a 9x5 pan. Put the sugars in a mixing bowl and mix together. Add in oil and applesauce and mix. Then, add 1 egg at a time, continuing to mix. Add vanilla. Mix all together. Add in grated zucchini and mix. Next, add all the dry ingredients and mix. Fold in nuts. Pour the mixture into a pan and bake for 50 to 55 minutes or until a toothpick comes out clean. Let cool and take out of the pan.

Makes 8 to 10 slices.

Made in the USA
Middletown, DE
30 November 2021